U0127373

歲次壬申年初秋
陳一郎 藏書.

Last Ship Home

Rodney Matthews

Paper Tiger

Paper Tiger Books
An imprint of Dragon's World
Limpsfield
Surrey RH8 0DY
Great Britain
First published by Dragon's World 1989
Reprinted 1991
© Dragon's World 1989
© Text by Nigel Suckling, Rodney Matthews 1989
© Illustrations Rodney Matthews 1989

No part of this book may be reproduced, or transmitted in any form or by
any means, electronic or mechanical, including photocopy, recording or
any information storage and retrieval system, without permission in writing
from Dragon's World Ltd, except by a reviewer who may quote brief
passages in a review.
All rights reserved.
Caution: All images are copyrighted by Rodney Matthews.
Their use in any form without prior written permission from
Rodney Matthews is strictly forbidden.

British Library Cataloguing in Publication Data
Matthews, Rodney *1945–*
  Last ship home
  1. English illustrations. Matthews, Rodney 1945–
  Illustrations
  I. Title
  741'.092'4
ISBN Hardback 1 85028 096 7
       Limpback 1 85028 095 9

Designed by Rodney Matthews
Typeset by Tradespools Ltd, Frome, Somerset
Printed in Singapore

CONTENTS

Although it might seem premature for this second volume of Rodney Matthews' to appear only four or five years after the publication of *In Search of Forever*, it is appropriate, as his work has undergone considerable changes from the time, back in 1974, when I first received some rather muddy colour prints at the Big O offices in London.

What excited me then, and developed into a mutually rewarding, creative relationship, was being led into a world that my academic education had ignored — a world where the people and the creatures of the past had booked their passage on the 'Starship Enterprise' bound for distant galaxies but had stopped off in Mesopotamia in the year 1215!

Afterwards I discovered such things as 'science fantasy', 'sword and sorcery', and even darker things. Rodney became one of the stars of our little galaxy, along with Roger Dean and others, but I never felt that Rodney was merely a part of that genre. It was as if he too had boarded the ship to an unknown destination.

Popular acclaim and great commercial success during the 1970s were initially what any artist would have settled for, but they only led Rodney further in his search for his real purpose as an artist. There were times when he might have felt that he was straying from the path, taking on work out of necessity rather than inspiration, and seeing inferior talents receive acclaim at a time when budgetary considerations often took precedence over artistic achievement.

This book, however, charts a resurgence, not only of his talent but the desire of others to commission and see his work published. With future projects such as 'Lavender Castle' which, hopefully, will become truly three-dimensional, we will find that *Last Ship Home* heralds the beginning of a great new endeavour.

Peter Ledeboer
February 1989

SECTION 1

INTRODUCTION

RODNEY MATTHEWS

HIS WORKING ENVIRONMENT

Rodney Matthews was born in the village of Paulton, Somerset, in 1945 and lived in or around there for the next forty years.

His father Jack, a multi-talented man, was a major influence on his early artistic development and also introduced him to the work of Walt Disney, who remains Rodney's main artistic hero to this day.

Another major influence was the countryside and wildlife by which he was surrounded. It was on the strength of a small portfolio of bird drawings that he was accepted by the West of England College of Art a while after leaving school. From there he served a rather gruelling apprenticeship with a well-established advertising agency, before setting up an outfit of his own with a friend, Terry Brace, which they called Plastic Dog Graphics.

In the early 1970s, by dint of perseverance almost as much as talent, he gradually broke into the fields for which he has become famous — posters, book covers and record sleeve design — and made forays into several neighbouring territories. In all this he was greatly helped by the patronage and encouragement of Peter Ledeboer who then commanded the enormously successful Big O poster company.

Since the publication of his first book, *In Search of Forever* (1985), Rodney has uprooted himself and his family and moved to North Wales. His lovely rambling farmhouse is perched high on a hill on the edge of the Snowdonia National Park, where the tranquillity is broken only by the occasional sheep or screaming jet fighter practising low-level flying overhead — a small price to pay for the abundant wildlife and stunning views.

For this volume, Rodney has produced a body of work with a distinctly different flavour from his last. 'Mellow' is a dangerous word to apply to it, since in art this is usually interpreted as 'clapped out', but it is one that comes to mind all the same, along with 'rich, humorous' and even (sometimes) 'joyful'.

A fascination with nature has always been apparent in Rodney's work, but on the whole it is the darker side of nature which dominates his best-known pieces. Recently the balance seems to have shifted, and the qualities which now radiate from many of his pictures are those which have hitherto been confined mainly to his early or peripheral work. Chief among them, in my estimation, is humour.

What is also clear from the new work is that he is still far from complacent about his technical skill, though it has long since passed a level most artists would envy. A characteristic of Matthews' compositions is their overall tone dominated by a single colour, most commonly from the blue-green end of the spectrum, a trick he learned from Walt Disney's work. This still holds but is now achieved by using a far wider range of colours, which lends a new richness and three-dimensional quality to the pictures. See for example 'The Walrus and the Carpenter' (p. 28) and 'Rivendell' (p. 16).

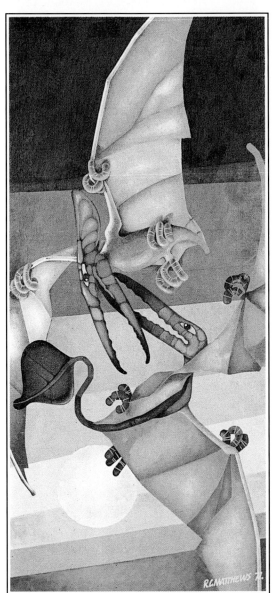

1. WALKING MISSILE LAUNCHER
1957 Poster colour

2. WEBLEY AIR PISTOL
1961 Gouache

3. PTERODACTYLS
1971 Acrylic gouache

Here are some early samples of work to demonstrate the budding Matthews style. Making allowances for technique, many such designs would sit quite comfortably beside much more recent work. Of them he says:

1) 'I produced this around 1957 at school (Paulton Secondary Modern). It was painted on that awful grey sugar paper they used to hand out, and with powder-type poster colours. It depicts a walking missile launcher which might almost have been appropriate a couple of decades later for *The Return of the Jedi*.'

2) 'This was painted as part of a commercial design course at art college, using gouache on art board. The gun itself (a Webley Senior air pistol) was often used by me for the untidy removal of panes of glass from my father's outbuildings!'

3) 'The pterodactyls were painted with acrylics on primed canvas during the period of my prehistoric fetish. The original is owned by Mr D. Bevan.'

BLUE PLANET SERIES 1974 Water colours

Above are two spreads from a series of four children's board books Rodney produced for Child's Play International in 1974. The original artwork was never returned (as was the norm in those days). The story, told in a purely visual way, concerned two children who built their own spaceship and flew to a blue planet in search of adventure.

The drawing below was a suggestion to the same company for a series of board books titled *Insect Antics*. Among the characters were an earwig opening a can of beans with its tail, and a spider knitting with the help of a stag beetle holding wool in its antlers. Unfortunately, the project was never realized.

INSECT ANTICS 1974

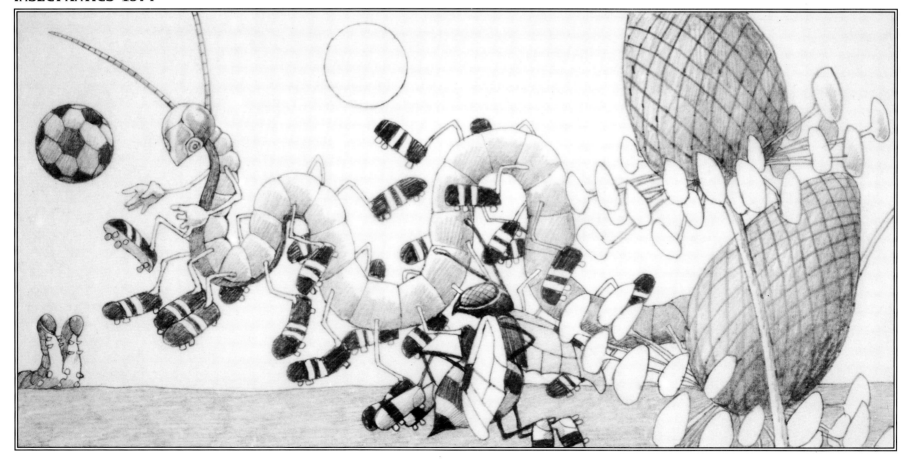

SHELOB 1973 Inks and tech. pen

OCTOPUS 1984 Inks

Above are two test pieces, one showing Frodo and Sam meeting Shelob in the pass into Mordor (from *Lord of the Rings*), the other for a proposed Harlech Television production called *Tales of Wonder* which never materialized. The octopus was to be electronically imposed on various backgrounds by a blue-screen technique, hence the dark-blue background to illustration.

Below is shown the development of the illustration 'An Unlikely Hero', which appears on p.17. Rodney experimented with a photographic 'out of focus' effect for the background.

Shown here is a small selection from Rodney's vast stock of reference photographs which help enhance the realism of his creations. For example, the all-black wasp (opposite, lower left) may be compared with the creatures in 'The Fire-wagon' on p.88. The green grasshopper similarly influenced 'The Hop' on p.45, while the coastal scene (above, right) helped shape the background to 'The Walrus and the Carpenter' on p.28.

As is apparent from these examples, Rodney's aim is not to transfer these images directly into his own work at all, but to bend and stretch and exaggerate them to suit his own purposes. That is the essence of his method. The wildest flights of his imagination are usually triggered by what most would consider quite commonplace, even boring, features of the countryside.

SECTION 2

CALENDARS
&
POSTERS

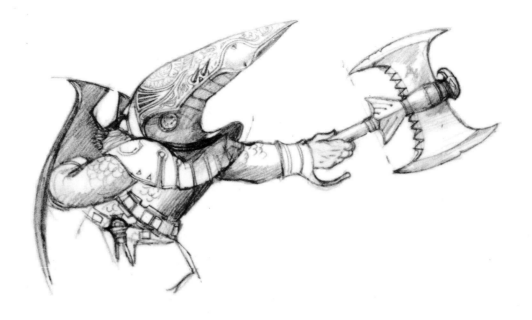

Rodney Matthews' big breakthrough came in 1974 when Big O in London began commissioning posters from him. Their swift popularity and rapid sales lifted his work out of obscurity and, it is probably fair to say, forged the basis of his fame.

Their sales now run to several million, and, although the Golden Age of Fantasy posters passed with the 1970s, they still form a large part of his work and still sell very well. Some titles, like 'Ilian of Garathorm', 'Tanelorn' and 'The Dragon Lord' have remained continuously in print since 1977, despite the demise of Big O, which must be some kind of record.

Currently his posters are published by (in alphabetical order) Anabas, Minerva, Picture Sales and Wizard & Genius.

The first Matthews calendar was published in 1978, featuring a set of twelve poster designs commissioned by Big O and illustrating various Michael Moorcock tales. Moorcock and Matthews already enjoyed a mutual professional regard, but this project led to a personal friendship which ultimately resulted in *Elric at the End of Time* — a book that Moorcock specifically wrote for him to illustrate, even shaping it around some Matthews ideas.

The first calendar, published by Big O in 1978 under the title *Wizardry and Wild Romance* bestowed on it by Moorcock, was successful enough to demand others which, in order of publication, were: *Another Time Another Place* (Big O, 1979), *Terrestrial Voyages* (Big O, 1980), *Mirador* (Mirador Pro-

ductions, 1983), *Transformation* (Picture Sales, 1985), *Dodecahedron* (Picture Sales, 1986), *Before and Beyond* (Picture Sales, 1987), *From Wondrous Tales* (Picture Sales, 1988), *Storybook Collection* (Picture Sales, 1990). Incidentally, the first calendar was published a year later in the United States.

Most of the calendars' themes are looser than the first because their main purpose was to display the best of a year's work from a variety of projects. The last two, however, were commissioned purposely as calendars, and allowed Rodney to choose his own theme. In the event, he chose to illustrate his favourite books, a marvellous freedom which must partly account for the fresh mood of the pictures.

This project also gave him the chance to do circular pictures for a change, encouraged by the success of a circular poster some years before. An unforeseen consequence of this is that the lack of a straight edge for the spiral binding has led them to become known in the trade as 'the loo seat calendars'.

It might be imagined that calendars are a rather transient way in which to package one's work, and that at the end of the year they will just be thrown away. In fact, Rodney finds that his have become collectors' items, thus justifying the time and care with which he assembles them.

**RIVENDELL-
THE LAST HOMELY HOUSE
1986** Inks 39cm dia.

Author: J.R.R. Tolkien
The Lord of the Rings
Publisher: Picture Sales

Author: J.R.R. Tolkien
The Hobbit
Publisher: Picture Sales

Author: J.R.R. Tolkien
The Silmarillion
Publisher: Pictures Sales

Author:
Sir Arthur Conan Doyle
The Lost World
Publisher: Picture Sales

Author: Jules Verne
20,000 Leagues Under the Sea
Publisher: Picture Sales

Author H.G. Wells
The War of the Worlds
Publisher: Pictures Sales

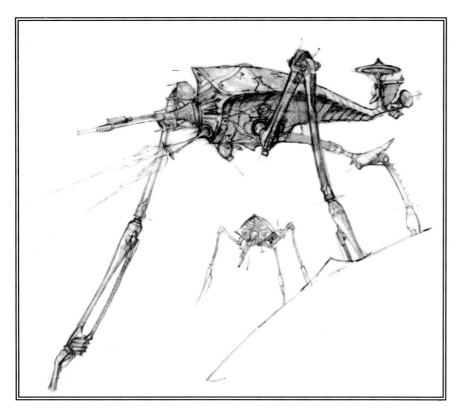

Preparatory drawing for 'The Martians'

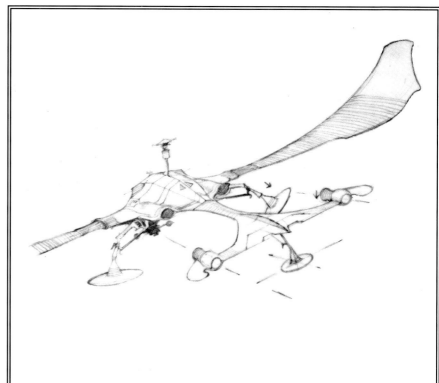

'The Duke to the Rescue'

Not surprisingly, pride of place in this series goes to scenes from Tolkien's three main books — *Lord of the Rings, The Hobbit* and *The Silmarillion.*

Matthews was slow in getting round to reading Tolkien, wary of the sudden wild acclaim Hobbits were receiving from people around 1970. Members of his band used to read *Lord of the Rings* on the way to gigs and complain about having to stop when they arrived at their destination. But when he did finally read the books, he fell in love with them as much as most people with a bent for fantasy and has since leapt at every chance to illustrate them.

Incidental snippets: the picture of Rivendell has been adopted for Matthews' letterheads and business cards because in spirit, if not in scale or detail, it bears a marked resemblance to where he now lives. The Mirkwood spider menacing Bilbo as he tries to rescue his friends was almost portrayed as a rare seven-legged variety because he had forgotten to add the last leg. Fortunately, this was spotted before it was too late. 'The Dwarves of Belegost' (p.18) has also appeared as a Magnum album sleeve.

For the next three, Matthews has chosen books from writers who might fairly be described as among the founding fathers of science fiction — Sir Arthur Conan Doyle, Jules Verne and H.G. Wells — all favourites of his youth.

'At the Pterodactyl's Roost' features his brother-in-law as the monster's target, which he swears is nothing personal. He just needed a model at the time to capture the pose.

'The Nautilus' and 'The Martians' have both featured in a Marshall Cavendish magazine series about great writers, along with the Edgar Rice Burroughs illustration 'The Sack of Zodanga' (p.40).

Many artists have tackled the Martians' theme over the years, so it was a challenge to produce a striking and original image. The buildings in the foreground are loosely based on Rodney's own outbuildings.

Author: Frank Herbert
Dune
Publisher: Picture Sales

TO STEAL A BATTLESHIP
1987 Inks 39 cm dia.

Author: E.E. 'Doc' Smith
Skylark of Valeron
Publisher: Picture Sales

Author:
Michael Moorcock
The Warlord of the Air
Publisher: Picture Sales

ALICE AND THE CATERPILLAR
1986 Inks 39 cm dia.

Author: Lewis Carroll
Alice's Adventures
in Wonderland
Publisher: Picture Sales

Author: Lewis Carroll
The Hunting of the Snark
Publisher: Picture Sales

THE WALRUS AND THE CARPENTER
1987 Inks 39 cm dia.

Author: Lewis Carroll
Publisher: Picture Sales

28

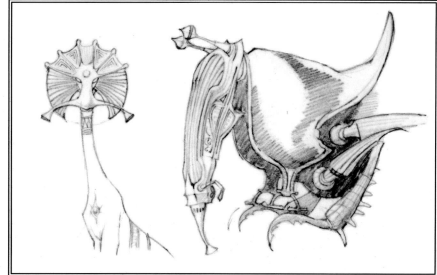

preparatory drawings The Tower of Flints

The Hall of Bright Carvings

Matthews was rather disappointed by the film of Frank Herbert's *Dune*, so p.23 shows how he would have handled some of the machinery, given the chance. The ornithopter received particular care because he would love to see an aeroplane based more closely on real birds.

Following this are two more flying machines. Rodney confesses that *Skylark of Valeron* is not really one of his favourite books, but he wanted to do a spaceship and it was the first suitable story that came to hand.

Moorcock's *War Lord of the Air* was chosen on stronger grounds, being a lively and imaginative tale about a parallel world which has evolved rather differently from our own. For instance, the year in which it is set is 1973.

Stronger still was the attraction of doing some Lewis Carroll illustrations (pp26–28) because a lasting impact was made on him at the age of seven or eight by Walt Disney's film of *Alice*. Any direct influence, though, must be subliminal because he can remember few of the details, only the overall mood.

Another influence may be Arthur Rackham, whose illustrations Rodney greatly admires and to which his own Alice clearly owes more than to Tenniel's better known depiction of her as a rather chubby, solemn-eyed girl.

In 'The Bellman and the Butcher' Matthews has made bold to suggest a possible answer to the eternal question, 'But what kind of creature was the Snark exactly?' For this he drew on some suggestions in his annotated version of the poem.

Mervyn Peake (detail left and following pages) is another of Matthews' heroes. He admires the man not only for his magnum opus, the *Gormenghast* trilogy but for his nonsense poems and artwork.

The great tragedy of Peake, apart from his dreadful last illness, was that his work only received its due recognition after his death. The *Gormenghast* books were well enough received by the critics when they appeared but they flopped, more or less, in the marketplace. His anguish at this is reflected, perhaps, in the character Crabcalf in *Titus Alone* — an invalid whose bed in the dim, dank cavern of the Under-River is surrounded by stacks of his great novel published thirty years before, of which only twelve copies had ever sold.

Peake says of him: 'He lay with his past beside him, beneath him and at his head: his past, five hundred times repeated, covered with dust and silver-fish. His head, like Jacob's on the famous stone, rested against the volumes of lost breath. The ladder from his miserable bed reached up to Heaven. But there were no angels.'

Sometimes *Titus Alone* seems less a continuation of the other two books then a dreamlike account of Peake's own search for a place in the world where he could find peace.

THE TOWER OF FLINTS
1988 Inks 39 cm dia.

Author: Mervyn Peake
Titus Groan
Publisher: Picture Sales

Author: Mervyn Peake
Titus Groan
Publisher: Picture Sales

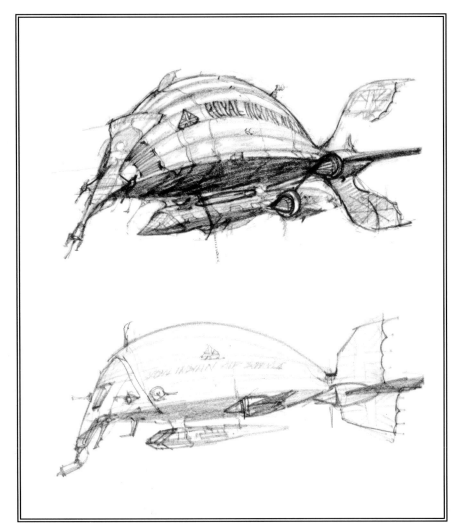

Preparatory drawings The Pericles

Page 33 The Dufflepuds Made Happy

'The Dufflepuds Made Happy' (opposite and p.34) was chosen for the Benson & Hedges Gold Awards' travelling exhibition in 1988, beginning at Hamilton's Gallery, London, before touring the country.

Exhibitions are not that common a feature of an illustrator's life, but Rodney has had a few. His book, *In Search of Forever*, was launched in 1985 with one at the Langton Gallery, London, attended by, among others, a hornet as big as a budgie which looked like it had escaped from one of the pictures. Or perhaps it was only looking to have its portrait painted.

In 1986 he was guest of honour at BD (Bande Dessinée) '86, an international festival of illustrators in Sierre, Switzerland, where he was given a large hall for a one-man show. The following year he featured with several other artists on the Dragon's World stand at the Brighton *Conspiracy* '87 world science fiction convention.

Such exhibitions are not usually great money-spinners but, as with book-signing sessions, they do give Matthews a chance to meet some of his usually anonymous admirers (which can be as embarrassing as it is flattering). Often they are also indirectly useful in attracting new commissions.

The attraction of 'The Wind in the Willows' (p.37) is that it reminds Rodney of that mood in childhood which exists before one realizes the shortcomings of the world; before, in current terms, one learns about holes in the ozone layer, the greenhouse effect and the possibility of nuclear disaster. There are perils in the book but they are only interruptions to an existence that is basically comfortable and assured.

THE DUFFLEPUDS MADE HAPPY
1986 Inks 39 cm dia.

Author: C.S. Lewis
The Voyage of the
Dawn Treader
Publisher: Picture Sales

Author: C.S. Lewis
The Silver Chair
Publisher: Picture Sales

Author:
Kenneth Grahame
The Wind in the Willows
Publisher: Picture Sales

Author: Edward Lear
The Owl and the Pussy-Cat
Publisher: Picture Sales

Publisher: Picture Sales

Author:
Edgar Rice Burroughs
A Princess of Mars
Publisher: Picture Sales

Author: Jack Vance
The Planet of Adventure
Publisher: Picture Sales

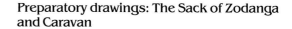

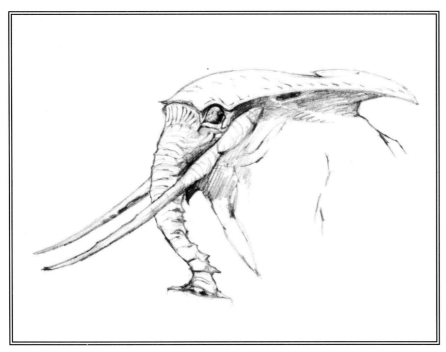

Matthews is often asked how one gets started as an illustrator, to which there are many answers, but he does not include going to art college. Although he did himself and enjoyed the experience, he does not see it as essential because he did not learn anything there that he could not have picked up elsewhere. Nor did he work very hard. That came later when he joined the advertising agency and his real education began.

Technical skill is needed to a high degree in this field, of course, but Rodney believes it can be acquired single-handedly provided you have enough perseverance and study the competition.

And an airbrush? Well yes, that is necessary up to a point, but Matthews, in fact, has an uneasy relationship with his and uses it less than most people imagine. For skies and misty effects, when he uses transparent ink, it is essential, but his pictures are mostly hand-painted with fine brushes — hence the textures he obtains. Too much airbrushing in a picture gives it a synthetic appearance — only acceptable if that is the nature of the subject.

Often he even hates the machine, but is forced to live with it, rather like, he says, the snake and rat who share a hole and find, after a while, that they can't live without each other.

The trouble is that when using the airbrush he can't relax. Nor can he forget the occasions when, in putting the finishing touches to a picture, the machine has splattered all over it. However, without changing to oils or acrylics, there is no immediate alternative.

'The Finale' (opposite) illustrates a poetic book of the same name by Calvin Miller, the concluding part of a trilogy based on the Gospels, the Book of Acts and, in this case, the Book of Revelation.

The story is an allegorical fantasy about the end of the world, the chaining of evil and the beginning of life on a new world free from death and suffering for those who survive the great war described in the book.

Rodney would like to do more of such work and has plans to do some Bible illustrations, but is likely to confine himself to the books of Daniel and Revelation which are in keeping with his style.

The cover of the book you are holding, incidentally, is a step in this direction. It illustrates no exact passage of scripture but is a personal statement by Matthews of his belief that this earthly life is only a temporary arrangement. The two contrasting pictures are likely to be published in tandem soon as a poster.

Author: Calvin Miller
Publisher: Picture Sales

PEACE . . . AT LAST
1985 Inks 42 × 30 cm
Publisher: Picture Sales

Despite the optimism of 'Peace at Last', Rodney does not believe that lasting peace on Earth is possible while man looks to himself for salvation.

However, for the tank depicted here he cast around for a creature of similar temperament and picked on the scorpion — the existing tank of this name was not his starting point —

which needed only slight modification to fit the purpose. A nice touch is the audacity of the doves who have made their nests in the gun barrels.

The picture was commissioned by Picture Sales for the 1986 calendar and has since been published as a mini-poster.

THE HOP
1985 Inks 44 × 28 cm
Publisher: Picture Sales

'The Hop' shows a common Matthews theme, prompted by his musical interests as much as anything else (such as the picture being required for a record sleeve), of which more will be said later. The picture also provided an opportunity to exercise his fascination with the minute and largely un-noticed life of insects, which he often finds as dramatic and puzzling as any human drama.

The drummers, incidentally, required no exaggeration beyond being supplied with hands. They are fairly exact representations of Katydid grasshoppers.

Preparatory drawings for The Hop

Looked at from an insect's level, the world is as vast and perilous as any fantasy scenario. Rodney once came across a large garden spider about to attempt a crossing of the North Circular road in London. He rescued it but was left wondering, 'Why?' Was the creature just incredibly stupid, or was it trying to reach some insect equivalent of King Solomon's Mines on the other side?

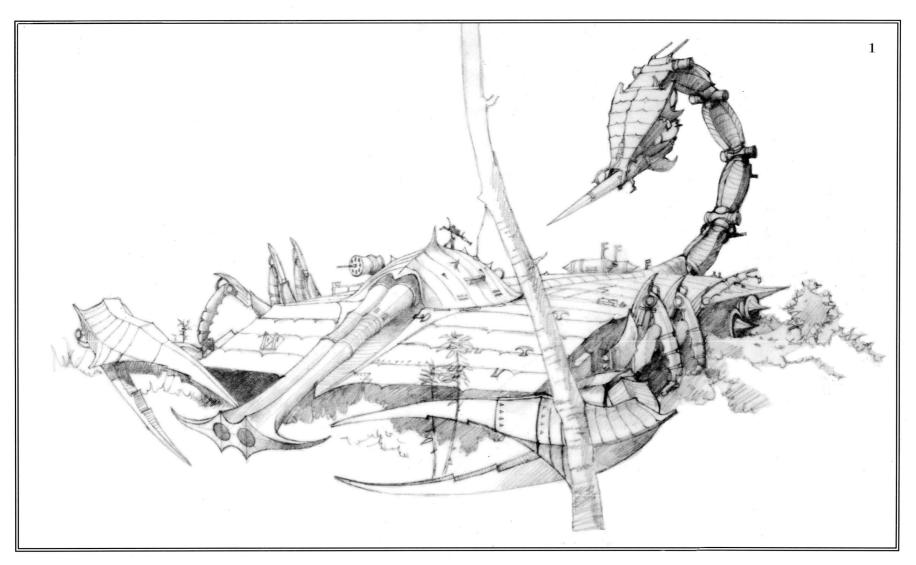

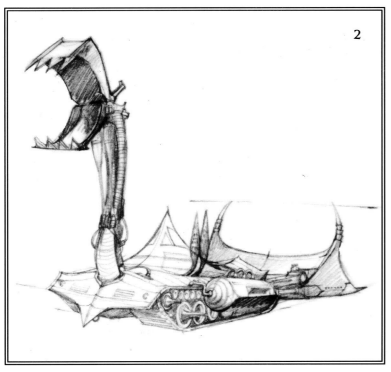

Preparatory drawings for
1 Peace at Last
2 £olly & $ons
3 Muzzlehatch and the Beast

SITE ACQUIRED
FOR DEFILEMENT
BY
£olly & $ons

£OLLY & $ONS
1985 Inks 33 × 23 cm
Publisher: Picture Sales

Page 49 MUZZELHATCH AND THE BEAST
1986 Inks 70 cm sq.
Author: Mervyn Peake   Publisher: Picture Sales

The picture above was requested by a publisher, but also happens to be a Matthews preoccupation. It presented a chance to vent his feelings about what he sees as the human rape of the planet, through greed as much as warfare (illustrated earlier). This picture echoes the sentiment of 'Stop the Slaughter', Rodney's blast against whale-hunting which appeared in his first book.

Opposite is a scene from *Titus Alone* by Mervyn Peake. The car is based on Rodney's own Lotus 7 whose temperament is not unlike that described by Peake. Isn't there a paradox be-

tween environmental concern and owning a car more lively than a Citroën 2CV? Matthews confesses that there is, a bit. He does not believe in extravagant cars, for Christian as much as conservationist principles, but he also believes a car is a tool which should do its job well. Perhaps there is also a touch of nostalgia for the days when he didn't look beyond the pleasure of driving. Whatever the reason, he has no plans to replace his Lotus with a Porsche, nor yet to swap it for a gutless dustbin (as the 2CV has been rather unkindly described).

TRAVELLING SHOW
1988 Pencil sketch

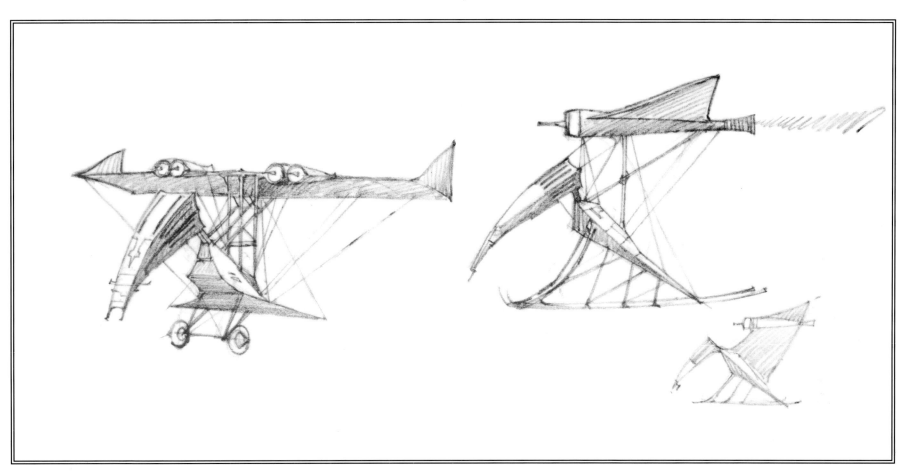

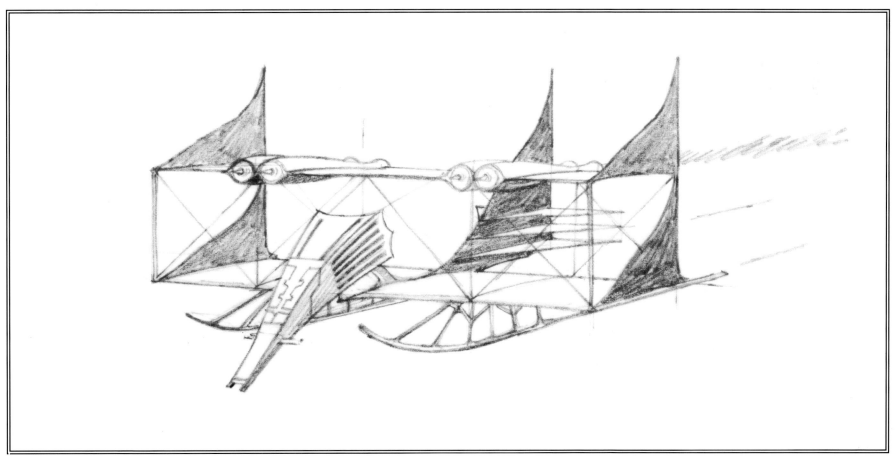

51

Page 51
preparatory drawings
for Dr. What?

DR. WHAT?
1985 Inks 29 × 42 cm
Commissioned by Coast
to Coast Productions
Publisher: Picture Sales

Pages 54 & 55
FOUR/FOUR AND FAST
1985 Inks 81 × 41 cm
Publisher: Picture Sales

THE TRUNK CALL
1985 Inks 42 × 52 cm
Publisher: Picture Sales

INTER-GALACTIC GAMES (Number one)
1986 Pencil sketch

'Travelling Show' on p.50 is a poster idea presented to Minerva showing a variation of a favourite Matthews' theme, which was not ultimately used. Following it are some aircraft designs, preparatory drawings for the 'Dr What?' picture on p.52.

This was part of a commission from Coast to Coast Productions for the conceptual design of a proposed *Dr Who* film. The picture originally featured Dr Who's famous Tardis hovering in front of the mantis-like machine, but when his own involvement in the project became uncertain, Matthews altered the design so it could be used in a calendar.

Such false starts in the film world seem almost the norm. In order to raise the vast sums of money involved, detailed 'packages' of ideas have to be assembled, an ingredient of which is often wild optimism.

So far Rodney has been involved in about five such ventures which have come to nothing. Although he is still keen to get involved in the film world, he is also getting wary of extravagant promises.

INTER-GALACTIC GAMES (Number three)
1986 Pencil Sketch

Following 'Dr What?' is a set of successfully approved and completed designs. Here and on the following page are three more proposal sketches for posters which were turned down in favour of other Matthews ideas presented at the same time.

Having ideas rejected can be a depressing experience if one forgets that it does not necessarily reflect on the quality of the idea itself. Art directors have other factors to take into account, such as whether they have an outlet for the idea or whether it meets the preconceptions of their client.

In the case of these three drawings, they may yet be completed some day more or less as they stand, but even when this is unlikely, Rodney always keeps such sketches because elements of them often come in useful for other ideas. An example of this appears later in the book.

ALL SEEING, ALL KNOWING
1988 Pencil Sketch

The sketch above was part of a batch of ideas requested by Wizard & Genius, who had detected a revival of interest in the kind of mystical themes popular in the 1970s and were looking for new images to fit. Such revivals are a regular cyclical occurrence as each new generation reacts against what has gone immediately before. It is not Matthews' original fans who keep his posters in print.

Rodney, as a Christian, is not interested in 'mysticism' as many people understand it — that is to say anything bordering on the occult, which to his knowledge can easily lead on to witchcraft and demonology. However, he did meet his customer's brief without compromising his faith.

The message here is one of God seeing and knowing everything that happens in the universe. Not, perhaps, in as visual a way as this eye in the sky, but in a complete and personal sense.

The sketch was submitted in the same batch of proposals as 'The Ether Stream' on p.60, of which more will be said in the appropriate place.

ALMOST HOME
1988 Inks 100 × 70 cm
Publisher: Anabas

'Almost Home' was commissioned by Anabas as a poster from a drawing like those we have just seen. It is a milder image than usual, with an innocence that almost belongs to the late 1960s or early 1970s, or to a child's bedroom wall.

Since the traumatic collapse of Big O in 1980, which at a blow wiped out most of his income, Matthews has avoided putting all his eggs in one basket. His posters still sell quite solidly, but through a variety of publishers. A useful consequence of this is that when one of them turns down an idea, it is quite often taken up by one of the others — as happened with 'Almost Home'.

Some ideas appeal to no one, of course, and these have to be relegated to the ideas file for future plundering.

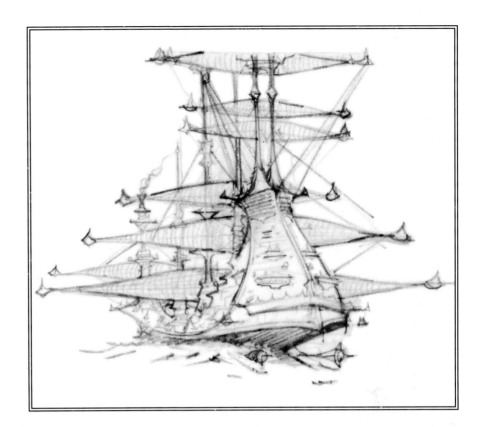

THE ETHER STREAM
1986 Inks 73 × 51 cm
Publisher: Wizard & Genius

Predicting the success of a picture is a perilous undertaking, particularly for the artist involved. Often the seemingly best ideas fall flat, while those which are knocked out almost absent-mindedly are greeted with wild enthusiasm.

Something like the latter happened to Rodney with 'The Ether Stream' for which the brief was fairly exact. The publishers had a poster of the Solar System which was selling rather well, so could he do something 'cosmic' and in the style of his early 1970s' pictures involving space and some planets?

With some misgivings he threw the requirements together, livening up the composition by deliberately introducing the red planet to jangle with the blue-green tones of the rest. He fully expected the result to be a damp squib, but in fact the poster has so far been very successful.

HIGH VELOCITY
1987 Pencil Sketch

Another consequence of having several publishers is the occasional spark of professional jealousy between them. One such occurrence prompted the sketch 'High Velocity' above. Fired by the strength and success of Matthews' '*Heavy Metal Hero*' poster (p.117) for Picture Sales, one of the others asked if he could produce something similar for them.

They were disappointed with the result and, on the whole, Rodney does not blame them. Sometimes, he feels, one should not try to repeat a success.

THE GRANITE CURTAIN
1988 Inks 100 × 70 cm
Publisher: Anabas

Page 64 Granite Curtain detail

The idea for 'The Granite Curtain' sprang from a lyric Rodney wrote for his band in about 1970. It went: 'They knew how to live, did they know how to die? Long granite curtains came down from the sky.'

At first glance the verse does not seem to be describing anything like the picture at all. Nor does it on the second or third glance for that matter. It was just the phrase 'granite curtain' that did the trick. This is quite a common Matthews mode of inspiration. Snatches of old songs pop into his head

to prompt new pictures that are usually quite different from the original imagery.

Rodney does not rate his own lyric-writing very highly, but it is plain from the titles of his pictures, calendars and books that he has an ear for a ringing phrase.

To emphasize that the rippling wall with its precariously balanced civilization is separating two different and mutually hostile worlds, deliberately clashing colours were chosen for either half of the picture.

The sketches on this and the previous page are unused ideas
for various posters which may yet be helpful for future projects. Such snippets also often come in useful for logos.

SECTION 3
BOOKS
&
MAGAZINES

Shortly after his first success with fantasy posters, Matthews broke into the field of book jacket illustration, starting with a cover for Michael Moorcock's *The End of All Songs*. When the trilogy of which it was part later appeared in one volume as *The Dancers at the End of Time*, the same picture was used.

This first commission arose from Moorcock's direct suggestion to the publishers, and led to many more for Moorcock himself and other writers, such as A. Merritt, André Norton, Clark Ashton Smith and Patricia McKillip.

Matthews' covers, particularly the Moorcock ones, continue to enjoy great success abroad, especially in Germany and the US, but he chooses to produce fewer these days. At one time he used to devour mountains of fantasy and SF, so was delighted to be working on such books, but these days he prefers to spend time reading the Bible whose stories are not only amazing but, he believes, true.

However, Matthews' interest in book projects demanding more than just a picture for the cover is as keen as ever. Fully illustrated books have been an ambition from the beginning, the first real fruit of which was Rodney's children's book *Yendor*, conceived in 1973 and published in 1978 by Big O. Next came his joint venture with Michael Moorcock, *Elric at the End of Time*, followed by a commission from Archival Press in the US to illustrate their edition of Moorcock's *Stormbringer*, though it is uncertain if this was ever published. Recently there have been his books of myths and legends about which more will be said in a moment.

Samples of these and a couple of other partially fulfilled projects will be considered here, along with a few other book and magazine illustrations, but first let us consider a slight mystery of the publishing world.

Fully illustrating a story from start to finish is a natural ambition for an artist, but such books are notoriously chancy for publishers unless they fall within certain well-defined categories. Unfortunately, adult fiction, even of the fantasy or science fiction variety, does not fit.

Why not? Considering the visual age we live in and the popularity of films, television, magazines and anthologies of illustration such as this, why do adults not want their novels perked up by occasional pictures? As anyone who has read a decent edition of Charles Dickens will know, it was once quite common, so why the big taboo now? Or is it just a fallacy? Anyone with an affirmative answer to the last question please send it on a postcard to your nearest large publishing house!

Opposite is an example from two sets of pictures commissioned by Usborne Publishing, London: eleven for a book of Greek myths and legends, and fifteen for a Norse equivalent. It is the only one Rodney is happy to show because by the end of the project he had grave doubts about it. This was partly because of the way his pictures were broken up by large white panels of text, but mainly because of the subject matter itself.

He says: 'As far as I was concerned at the beginning, the

THE FORGING OF THE TREASURES
1986 Inks 56 × 37 cm
Publishers: Usborne & Picture Sales

stories were no more than myth, so could be tackled like any other form of fantasy. But later I learned that these "gods", particularly the Norse ones, are still worshipped in occult circles and I have no wish to be associated with them.'

His wariness of the occult now also extends to role-playing and fighting fantasy games, for which he has executed some pictures in the past. Some are harmless enough, he says, but many involve nothing less than witchcraft. This conviction comes from more or less first-hand experience, as he has one Christian friend who ministers to youngsters disturbed by such games, as well as by Tarot cards and Ouija boards, and another friend who was a prominent black witch.

A SONG FROM THE LOCKER
1985 Inks 52 × 37 cm
Commissioned on behalf of
Kerrang! rock magazine
(unused)
Published by Picture Sales

EARL AUBEC OF MALADOR
1984 Inks 26 × 37 cm
Author: Michael Moorcock
Imagine Magazine cover
Publisher: TSR Hobbies (U.K.)

AR-CE-EM 242
1986 Inks 26 × 37 cm
Publishers: Orbit magazine (Holland)
and Picture Sales

BENEATH THE WALL
1986 Inks 28 × 42 cm
Author: Joseph O'Neill
Land Under England
Publisher: Penguin Books

ELRIC AT THE END OF TIME (Front cover)
1982 Inks 26 × 37 cm
Author: Michael Moorcock
Publisher: Paper Tiger

MEANWHILE, BACK TO THE BATTLE
1980 Inks 26 × 36 cm
Author: Michael Moorcock
Publisher: Paper Tiger

The large number of covers and posters Matthews produced for Michael Moorcock's books in the 1970s culminated in the book *Elric at the End of Time,* which was written specifically for him to illustrate and shaped to some extent around his suggestions. It was published by Paper Tiger in 1987 and contains twenty-two colour illustrations and eleven monochrome drawings.

Elric is one of Moorcock's most famous warrior heroes,

despite being a rather tragic and unfulfilled character possessed of very equivocal moral values. The story tells of how he is transported to a whimsical world at the end of time whose inhabitants can conjure almost any fantasy with a touch of their power rings. They mean him no harm — in fact, quite the contrary — but he becomes convinced he has fallen into the power of the Lords of Chaos and wants only to escape back to his own time and plane.

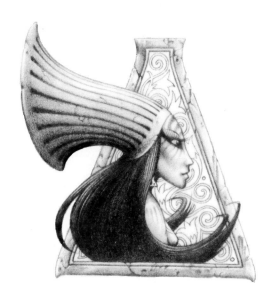

Elric at the End of Time

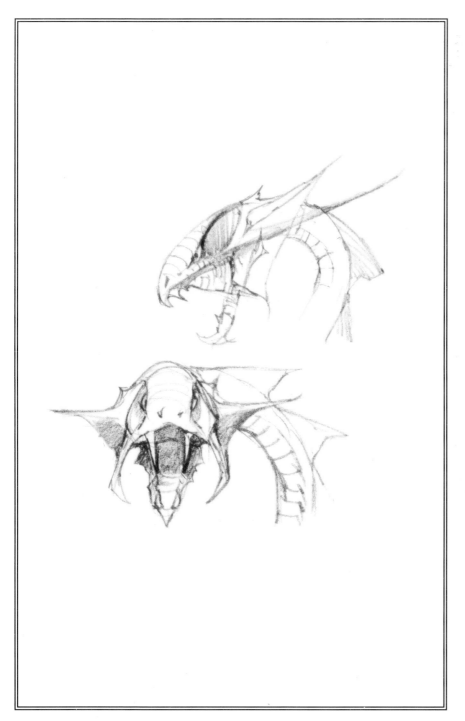

Page 76 IN SEARCH OF FOREVER (Redrawn version)
1984 Inks 39 cm sq.
Publisher: Paper Tiger

SEAS OF BLOOD
1985 Inks 27 × 36 cm
Publisher: Puffin Books
Also French, Spanish, Japanese and US editions

Opposite is a redrawn version of Rodney's 1974/5 poster 'In Search of Forever' produced for his book of the same name. The redrawing was undertaken partly to match the proportions of the book, partly to apply more sophisticated techniques to a favourite image.

The picture above was commissioned by Penguin for the cover of a fighting fantasy book about pirates on the high seas. The story seemed harmless enough in itself, but for reasons given earlier Rodney feels uneasy about having had anything to do with the genre.

'The Fury' (overleaf) owes its title to the pace at which it was produced, as much as its subject. To meet a deadline it was finished in three days.

THE FURY
1988 Inks 33 × 46 cm
Magazine Advertisement
Publisher:
Software Communications

78

WORLDS WITHOUT WORDS
1987 Inks 30 × 43 cm
Publisher: 4Mation
Educational Resources

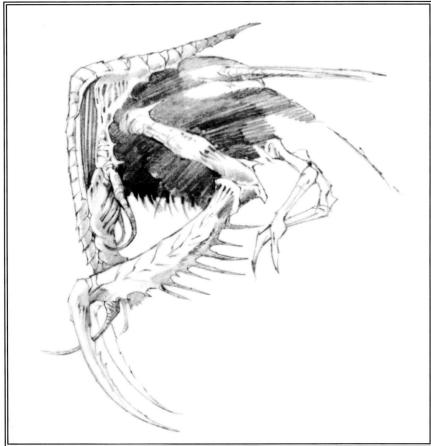

Preparatory drawings for The Moth & the Moon

Pages 84 & 85
CROSSING THE DESERT
1986 Inks 64 × 33 cm

THE LEAVETAKING
(Redrawn version)
1987 Inks 39 cm dia.

KOYOTUMA
1984 Inks 41 × 26 cm

Page 87 DRUMTOWER
1984 Inks 38 cm sq.

This project, 'The Moth and the Moon', began for Rodney in about 1973 with a suggestion by a friend that they make a semi-animated film based on his pictures. He rapidly produced about fifty pictures, but the scheme fell into abeyance for various reasons, including the demand for Matthews' posters and book covers. Some of the pictures were published as cards and posters by Big O but the rest languished for several years until, taken by the style of my first

novel, he approached me with the suggestion that I try and weave a story around the material.

This I duly did, while he began a fresh set of illustrations. The first version of the novel was complete about the time *In Search of Forever* was published, since when its peregrinations round the London publishing houses have been almost as arduous and eventful as its hero's. Whether they will share the same ultimate fate remains to be seen.

THE FIREWAGON
1987 Inks 100 × 70 cm

The story concerns a young prince, heir to the throne of his dying father, whose kingdom is suddenly threatened by an enemy whose very existence has been forgotten in the land. Before the true scale of the threat dawns on the rest of the country, he is told of a prophecy concerning his time, one which demands the 'unforgetting' of many things and a mission into the Outer World to heal the wound of an ancient wrong, leaving his kingdom to fend for itself as best it can. For, it is said, the Kingdom of Talassar can by its own strength do no more than postpone its day of ruin.

With little more than this prophecy to give him confidence, he sets off into the forgotten world beyond Talassar's encircling mountains, a world where the very laws of possibility are different and humans have long been losing their battle for survival. And there he finds…well, he finds that his prophecy is often a pretty slender foundation for hope. Let's leave it at that.

STRONGHOLD
1987 Inks 100 × 70 cm

People have often asked of this collaboration, 'But in the end whose story is it?' There is no simple answer. Broadly speaking, the beginning is Rodney's, since the bulk of his early pictures covered that part; the ending is mine, since it was left to me to bring the action to a head; and the middle is, well, a bit of both. But this is a great oversimplification.

What it often felt like was chipping away at some clay-encrusted statue from different angles. Occasionally our chisels met and we simultaneously uncovered some fresh aspect of the plot, more often we chipped away separately and pooled our discoveries from time to time till the work stood revealed.

In a sense we each now see it as our own project as much as a shared one, which is probably how it should be.

THE WALLED KINGDOM
1986 Inks 40 × 31 cm

What was remarkable about working on the project together was how few disagreements arose in the course of the main work. In fact, more have surfaced since then, partly because the story has continued to evolve gradually, partly because so have our separate views on whether it fulfils the original intention — to tell the tale of a spiritual quest rather than a blood-and-guts adventure. However, that, like the saga of finding an amenable publisher, is an ongoing story.

These new illustrations have appeared in some of Rodney's recent calendars, and 'Stronghold' has been published as a very successful poster.

One or two of the designs are reworkings of the original drawings to bring them up to the standard of more recent work but, to give a flavour of the project's starting point, a selection of other originals is shown on the next few pages.

Here, the hero, Tenaris, has the nature of his quest revealed to him by the King's Keeper of Secrets and is introduced to his chosen companion, a doughty warrior named Crem, who provides some compensation for the prince's youth and basic timidity. Tenaris is rather unpromising material for the bold venture before him, being of a rather withdrawn and passive temperament.

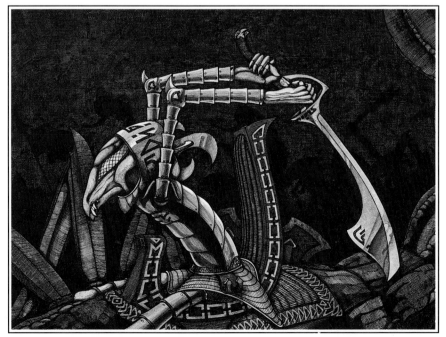

The scenes on this page did not feature in the book in the end, largely because of a need to hurry the story along at this point. The close sequence of the pictures was required by the original aim of semi-animation, which also explains why fifty pictures were not enough to delineate the whole tale.

THE SPUD SNUZZLER
1986 Water colours 59 × 33 cm

'A high velocity potato whistling through the air usually means that there is a Spud Snuzzler about. An attack seldom proves fatal, though coming spuddenly and from a low altitude is often extremely disturbing.

'This fast-flying spudnivore of the family Shootimus Spudimus Hardimus causes havoc among agricultural workers as they gather in the harvests from the fields. There appears to be no effective defence against these aerial forays, other than to wear a sturdy helmet and to return the fire using a cricket bat.

'If the Spud Snuzzler is unable to obtain stocks of its usual projectiles, it will happily fire other root vegetables, including turnips, parsnips and stout carrots, also, at a pinch, a short firm cucumber (though these are less accurate and cannot be used in rapid fire).

'Snuzzlers nest in vast colonies called "Snuzzleries", usually situated in tall trees near cultivated land where pickings are easy. The nest itself is constructed in a haphazard fashion from potato sacks and lined with farmers' "wellies" and cow dung.

'Their main food is, of course, potatoes, but the Snuzzler will change its diet to small mammals such as the Rot Rat or the Skulking Stench Weasel if potatoes are out of season, or have all been fired away in some pointless skirmish.

'The call of the Spud Snuzzler is a high-pitched bubbling noise, rather like someone trying to play a bugle whose end is immersed in a bucket of lukewarm porridge.'

THE RED RENDER VERSUS THE LOWER WARTLEROTTER
1978 Water colours 59 × 33 cm

Page 96 & 97 THE DARK MOULDERER
MEETS THE FESTERING FIRE-THROAT
(To his deep discomfort)
1987 Water colours 59 × 33 cm

Another long-running Matthews' project dating from 1977 is his *Field Guide to Nasties*, based on the long study he had made of the more obscure forms of British wildlife. So far, and at no small cost in cuts, bruises and severely tested sensibilities, he has tracked down and identified about thirty-five such varieties and, since his move to Wales, has begun extending the range to cover several peculiarly Cymruc varieties.

Some examples appeared in *In Search of Forever*, and five have recently been published as 'mega-prints' by Picture Sales, but for anything like a complete survey of such creatures the world will have to wait a while longer.

Matthews' deceptively simple texts are the careful distillation of mountains of laboriously collated notes which, due to the circumstances in which many were written, have begun to acquire a wildlife of their own which may necessitate an appendix or two to the completed opus.

THE OOMI GOOLY BIRD
1987 Water colours 30 × 33 cm

THE FLATULUS
1987 Water colours 30 × 33 cm

'Very few communities of small goblins, gnomes or wood sprites have escaped a frequent visit from this winged terror. It will eat anything up to one hundred small goblins or similar creatures in the course of a day's rampage and, when it is rearing its young, it can sometimes be seen struggling through the air with a great beakful of cursing unfortunates.

'The Oomi Gooly Bird builds a great, foul-smelling nest from regurgitated goblin armour and weapons at the very top of a high rock or cliff and therein lays just one egg, which takes all of three years to hatch, primarily because the bird cannot be bothered to sit on it very often.

'When it is hunting, the Oomi Bird tries to snatch its victim without having to land because it has no legs, making any heavy contact with the ground extremely uncomfortable. Every now and again the landing procedure cannot be avoided, whereupon it will shriek its well-known call, "Ooomi goolies, ooomi goolies", from which its name is derived.

'When it's not at the nest, the Oomi Bird will roost, or rather hang by the beak, from the tops of large forest trees among dense foliage. Its position is usually given away by the frustrated cussings of the half dozen or so uneaten goblins held between its ten-foot wings in readiness for a later feast, or by the huge pile of droppings under the tree. With all taken into consideration, this is a very unattractive creature which should be avoided like a plague of poison pimpled toads!'

THE TRIPLE SMATTER
1987 Water colours 30 × 33 cm

THE DEVIOUS DRAGONER
1987 Water colours 30 × 33 cm

The 'Nasties' pictures are done in watercolours instead of Matthews' usual inks. Partly this is just for a change, so he can experiment with obtaining different textures by saturating the paper to different degrees. The occasional randomness and overrunning of these effects does not matter because he is not aiming for a high degree of realism.

Partly it is just because filling in outline drawings with watercolour is quick work. These pictures usually take about two days, as opposed to a week or more using inks.

THE KILLWING

THE GREEN SERPENT

'It was, indeed, just as he had thought. Screaming down towards him from the ugly sky was an even uglier Killwing.

"Not bad for starters," cried Yendor in a small voice, and he raised his sword and shield in the first defensive position. He had learnt how to do this from his dad, but he wasn't too sure if it worked against Killwings. With his nerve failing and his eyes tightly shut, Yendor felt a great rush of air pushing him backwards off the edge of the cliff. The Killwing had missed!'

Rodney's children's book, *Yendor* (a name later bestowed on his son), was published by Big O in 1978, with a text by Graham Smith. It stars a young hero who, fired by the tales told by his adventuring father over dinner, decides to go out into the world to pick up a few tales of his own.

Girding on his Junior Adventurer outfit, he slips out of the house one night and sets off into the wild...

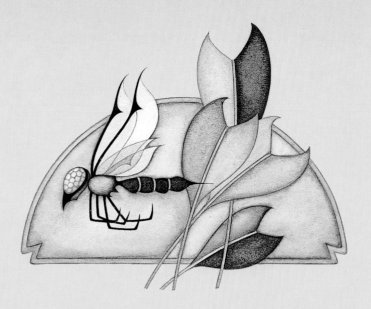

THE GRUMPOSAUR

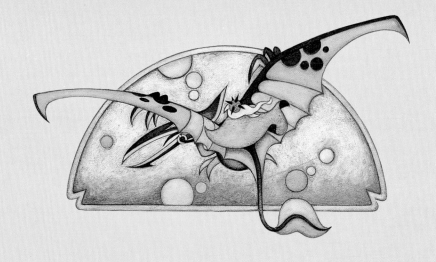

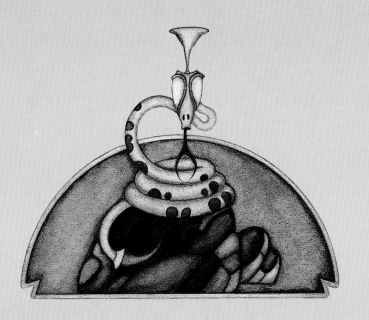

"GOOD MORNING"

Luckily for Yendor, half the adventures that might happen to him don't, and the other half aren't a bit as scary as they deserve to be. Then a friendly giant stops him going beyond the point of no return and offers him a lift home on a tame flying snawk. This suddenly seems a good idea, and so tired is Yendor from his adventures that he falls asleep on the way. The next he knows, he is unaccountably tucked up in bed and being woken by his mother who has just entered with a tray of breakfast.

SECTION 4
RECORD COVERS

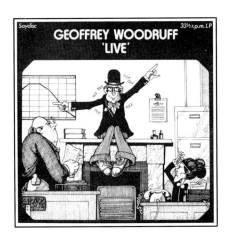 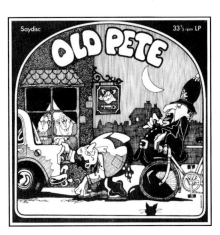 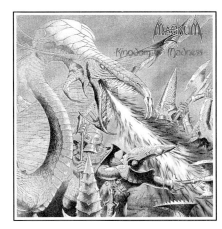 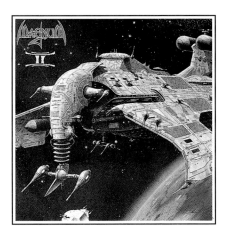

GEOFFREY WOODRUFF 'LIVE'
6″ LP
1974 Saydisc Records

OLD PETE
6″ LP
1974 Saydisc Records

KINGDOM OF MADNESS
Magnum
1988 FM Revolver Records

MAGNUM II
1988 FM Revolver Records

When asked to describe his style, Matthews occasionally describes himself as belonging to 'The seventies progressive rock album cover school' whose first notable exponent was Roger Dean with his powerful Osibisa and Yes album covers.

In fact, Rodney did not actually produce any such covers at the time. In the early 1970s his cover designs were mainly for folk-related bands, and at the end of the decade they were for more mainstream rock groups. The phrase is, nonetheless, apt because he was dealing with a kind of imagery that has come to be associated with progressive rock. At the time, he was also playing such music with his own band, so that is where his heart was. It was only because of always being in slightly the wrong place at the right time that he did not become involved.

Music means almost as much to Matthews as art. He says he often feels like a frustrated drummer chained to a drawing board, which perhaps explains the many weird and wonderful bands and orchestras which crop up in his paintings. Both interests can be traced back to childhood and the influence of his father, who was a dance-band drummer. For several years Rodney toured with rock bands of his own (the tale of whose adventures would make a hilarious, if unedifying, book) before deciding they were not, after all, going to break into the big time.

Later he was to reappear as a jazz drummer, keeping his hand in by playing with local bands around Bristol, and now North Wales (with the Cambrian Coast Quartet who, despite their name, feature anything between three and five players).

The shift is not as great as it may seem, though. Rodney says: 'After all, I have always liked jazz and even took lessons from a jazz drummer while playing rock in the early days. He used to get me playing coordinated independence from a Joe Morello drum tutor, which is not only hard on the wrists but hard on the brain. Actually Joe Morello is one of my favourite drummers, along with the likes of Gene Krupa, Buddy Rich, Connie Kay (Modern Jazz Quartet), and more recently Billy Cobham, Jon Hiseman and Bill Bruford.'

But the interest in rock is only lying dormant, along with the ambition to combine music and images. There is a Matthews plan brewing to revive both.

Incidentally, the logo for this section derives from an early 1970s poster (now lost) for a Bristol college gig. The original showed a strange little creature feeding sheet music into a machine, from the other end of which came speech bubbles holding the names of featured bands, such as The Strawbs and The Third Ear Band. In the new version the machine delivers (symbolically) the different kinds of music people want.

VAGABONDS OF THE WESTERN WORLD
Rough Sketch 1973 Markers and coloured pencils

VIGILANTE
Rough Sketch 1986 Gouache and ink

Page 108 ON A STORYTELLER'S NIGHT
1985 Inks 41 cm sq.
Magnum
FM Records

Page 109 TIGER MOTH
1984 Inks 35 cm sq.
Rogue Records

On the opposite page the two covers on the left are examples of early Matthews EP covers. On the right, by way of contrast, are two recent LP sleeves.

Above left is a rough visual done for the front of a Thin Lizzy album, *Vagabonds of the Western World*, in the early 1970s. It was rejected in favour of a Jim Fitzpatrick design, about which Rodney has no hard feelings because it was very fine. He was left to do only the graphic layout of the reverse.

Above right is another sleeve-that-never-was. The design was requested by the band but not used because of a change of record company. As it happened, Rodney was not too pleased with it himself and felt that with a looser brief he could have done better.

On the following page is one of Matthews' best-loved pic-

tures, 'On a Storyteller's Night', which was used by Magnum as a sleeve and published as a poster by Anabas. As surprising as the degree of lively detail is that it took only ten days to complete (with the help of some midnight oil).

The suggestion came from Tony Clarkin, Magnum's leader, writer and lyricist. The tavern's interior is faintly reminiscent of The George in Norton St Phillip near Rodney's former home in Somerset. Background details include two previous Matthews' covers for the band, while his own dog, Patch, is under the table.

Though he leads a more sober life now than in his dissolute youth, Matthews confesses that he still enjoys a quiet pint in such places, which must have contributed to the richness of the composition.

108

Same size detail from 'Sextet'

Page 110 SEXTET
1988 Inks 36 cm sq.
Tiger Moth (Title: Howling Moth)
Rogue Records

On pp109 and 110 are shown two Tiger Moth covers commissioned by Ian Anderson of Rogue Records (who also plays in the band and runs the magazine *Folk Roots*).

Tiger Moth is a folk-rock band which plays modern arrangements of traditional tunes. The first cover won first prize in the relevant section of the Music Trades' Association Awards 1984 and has also appeared in poster, postcard and calendar formats. The second, 'Sextet', is loosely based on 'The Hop' in the 1987 Matthews calendar. Its creatures are exaggerated versions of stock British insects, such as the cockchafer, weevil and earwig. The album was called *Howling Moth* (presumably drawing some parallel or contrast with Howling Wolf).

SANTUARY
1981 Inks 100 × 60 cm. (Record use 1986)
Motherlode
Active Music Productions

Page 112 Sextet pencil sketches

Not content with designing exotic instruments for the drummers in his pictures, Matthews recently decided it was perhaps time he tried making something a bit out of the ordinary for his own use. A prototype of part of the proposed drum kit is shown below left, and can be compared with the instruments in 'Drumboogie' (detail below), 'Sextet' (opposite and p.110), '4/4 and Fast' (p.54), 'A Song from the Locker' (p.70) and 'Drumtower' (p.87). The last is probably the most relevant example, but the others give a fair idea of what might follow if Rodney gets a taste for this kind of work.

The patterns for the drums were made of chipboard, hardboard and cellulose filler. Fibreglass moulds were then professionally made from these and in turn used to produce the drum shells, also in fibreglass. Fitted with standard heads, they produce a distinctly unusual sound, but unfortunately are a bit too cumbersome for playing jazz in rural venues, being more suited to large rock concerts.

For the future, it is possible that Rodney could find himself involved in projects centred on customized drum kits to order, his main contribution being their design. This could also be extended to other instruments like electric guitars. A further possibility is of introducing electronics to the drums, so that their natural sound can be shaped to produce any desired effect.

The earlier picture 'Sanctuary' (left) was requested for the cover of the first album release of Motherlode, a Swedish band managed by Matthews' friend Dennis Karlson. The album was given the title *The Sanctuary*.

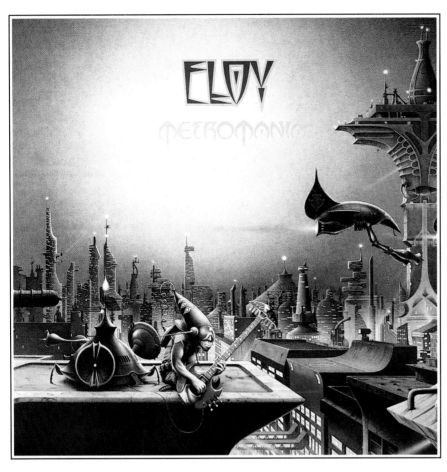

The *Metromania* sleeve on the left was taken from the original of Rodney's 'Be Watchful' poster without the superimposed face of Christ. It was requested by EMI for the German release, but was also used in Britain by Heavy Metal Records.

Below is a concept sketch submitted for an earlier Eloy album, *Planets*. It was turned down in favour of another Matthews design, but elements of it were used elsewhere — the aircraft in 'Be Watchful' and the floating fortresses in 'The Trunk Call' on p.53.

Page 115 AT THE BREAKING OF THE SEALS
(Revelation Ch 6)
1989 Inks 48 cm sq.
Full Moon
Voices of Wonder Records

METROMANIA
Eloy (Record use 1984)
EMI Records Germany and Heavy Metal Records U.K.

THE HEAVY METAL HERO **1985** Inks 100 × 70 cm
(Record use 1987)
Diamond Head
Am I Evil
FM Revolver Records

Page 118 MIRADOR
1981 Inks 100 × 60 cm.
(Record use 1987)
Magnum
FM Revolver Records

'At the Breaking of the Seals' (previous page) was produced for the cover of an album by the British band Full Moon. It was commissioned by Voices of Wonder Records in Norway who had no very exact idea of what they wanted, except that it had to be something to do with the moon. Rodney took advantage of this to pick a passage from the Book of Revelation which describes the moon turning to blood and the Four Horsemen of the Apocalypse being unleashed upon the Earth — an example of how this field sometimes makes it possible for an artist to please himself as much as his clients, since the band was well pleased with the result.

It is Rodney's belief that these horsemen are already in action — the white horse of conquest, the red horse of war, the black horse of famine and plague, and the pale horse of death.

Matthews became a Christian in 1980 but had been thinking about God for some ten years before, prompted by a Christian artist friend who had alarmed him with Bible prophecies of the last days. He quickly adds, however, that this does not mean he is a Jehovah's Witness.

As a result of being a Christian, Rodney finds he has to turn down a fair amount of record and video work on moral grounds, but finds he has yet to go hungry as a result. (God is no man's debtor!)

'Heavy Metal Hero' (opposite) is one of Matthews' most popular images and has appeared in several formats, as well as on the cover of a Diamond Head anthology album. It is true that both this and the following picture 'Mirador' appeared in Rodney's first book, but having been used since as album sleeves, it seems fair enough to show them again on a larger scale.

'Mirador', both picture and title, were adopted for a Magnum album by Paul Birch of FM (formerly Heavy Metal) Records, who also happens to be a Christian. ('Is nowhere safe?' I hear the heathen among you ask.)

116

SECTION 5

LETTERING
&
LOGOS

1

The letterhead above was commissioned by APB Process Print in Bristol, with whom Rodney has been dealing since the early 1970s. The picture is more or less a cross between 'Heavy Metal Hero' and 'Ether Stream', but with customized details like the register mark on the front, colour-coding in the smoke and the printing machine in tow.

1. APB Letterhead
2. 1990 Calendar
3. Mega-prints broad sheet

2

3

1

A B C D E F G H I J K
L M N O P Q R S T
U V W X Y Z & ? ! ( )
1 2 3 4 5 6 7 8 9 0

2

Rodney Matthews
1 2 3 4 5 6 7 8 9 0

1. Alphabet 'windsweep' 1984
2. W & G Poster broad sheet 1981
3 & 4. Album logos 1984
5. Game logo 1988

3

TIGER · MOTH

4

TIGER MOTH

TIGER MOTH

5

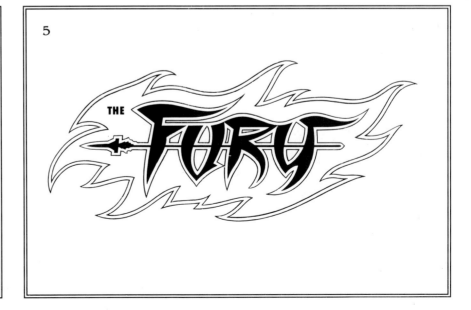

THE FURY

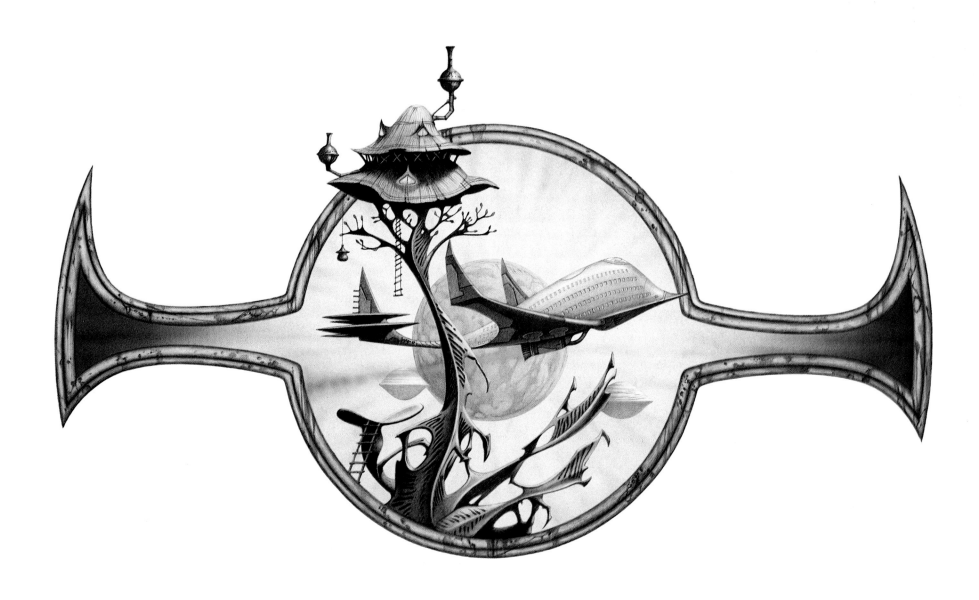

Picture sales: poster broad sheet logo No. 1 1988

Matthews' interest in lettering and logos goes back to art college where he learned the basics. The college exercises were in themselves rather tedious, but they provided the necessary framework to which he could later apply his imagination.

When he first entered the commercial world there was no such thing as instant dry transfers for lettering, so it usually had to be done by hand. Again, this was rather laborious at the time, but has come in useful since.

In the early 1970s his own agency, Plastic Dog Graphics, began producing letterheads and logos (mostly for companies and bands in the music business), and he has continued this line of work intermittently ever since. It is a sideline, but a very useful one because it means that when his work is to appear with lettering he can make sure it is sympathetic and well laid out.

Doing logos like the one above and on the opposite page is also a useful way of using up odd ideas which do not fit into any larger composition. These two were commissioned by Picture Sales for use on poster broadsheets.

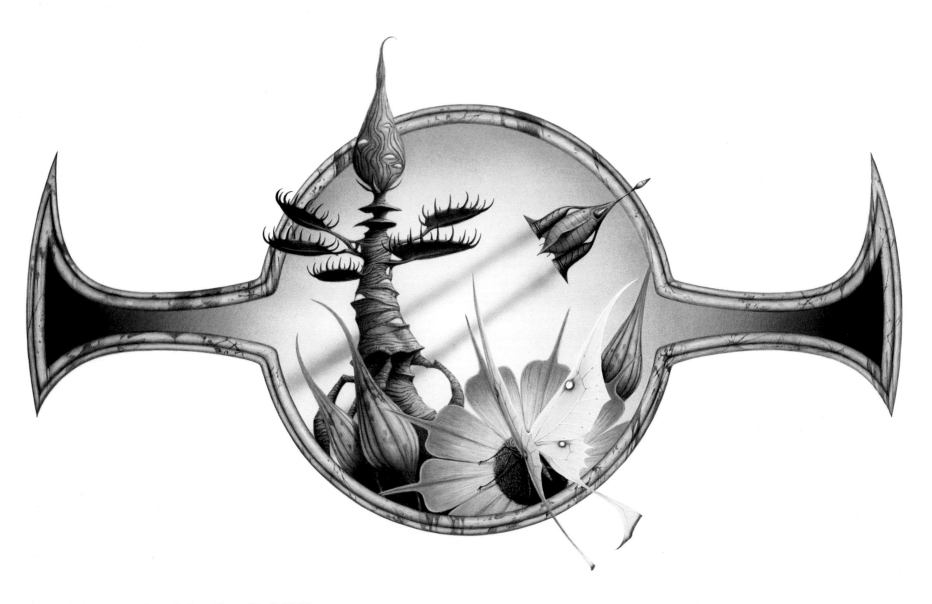

Picture Sales poster broad sheet logo No. 2 1988

Page 124   1. Educational Package 1987
2. Video tape box 1985
3. Pace-Minerva poster broad sheet 1983
4 & 5 1983 Calendar

There is a story behind all the logos, of course, but one which is particularly worth mentioning, since there was no room earlier, is 'World Without Words' on the next page. This went with the picture on p. 79 to form the box cover of an educational package for children produced by 4mation Educational Resources.

The aim of this package, masterminded and mostly written by Mike Matson, is to introduce children to the idea of communicating in ways other than those they are used to. This is achieved by creative projects centred on a computer game featuring an alien spaceship, posters, music, fantasy stories and a study on communicating with the deaf-blind.

Apart from doing the cover, which is reproduced as a poster inside, Rodney was asked to contribute a piece explaining his work and the ideas and motivations behind it.

123

1

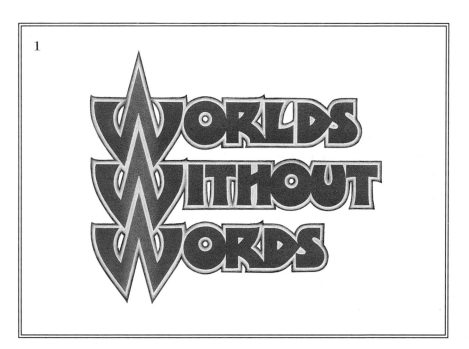

WORLDS WITHOUT WORDS

2

YOR

Rodney Matthews

4

February
August
October

5

December
1 2 3 4 5 6 7
8 9 0

1 & 2 Alternative
Eloy logos 1982
3 & 4 Pencil sketches
5 Dragons World logo

6 Record cover 1987
7 Book cover 1982

1 & 2 MCA Records
letterheads 1972
3 Shakin' Stevens
letterhead 1973
4 logo 1973
5 Band logo 1989

1

MOTHERLODE

2

The Sanctuary

3

4

5

6

7

BEFORE & BEYOND 1987

1 logo 1986
2 Record cover 1986
3 4 5 & 6 Unused logos 1986
7 1987 Calendar

This is something Matthews has been itching to get his teeth into for some time. He says, 'As with the "Granite Curtain" picture, this project arose from a rather juvenile lyric written for my band back when silly verses were fashionable.

'The song was entitled "Lavender Castle" and starred characters like Lady Forgetmenot and John Dory. It was all rather gentle stuff considering what a "yob" I was at the time.'

Although not too much is going to be revealed because of the notoriously light-fingered film business, the idea is basi-cally for an animated TV series featuring a strange and lov-able band of characters flitting about space in search of adventure and wrongs to right — a bit like an intergalactic Robin Hood and his merry men.

The Lavender Castle is their home base, the haven they retreat to from time to time to recharge their batteries. The details of their spacecraft are still classified but the interior view on p.131 gives an idea of Lavender Castle technology — proof that high-tech can also be homely.

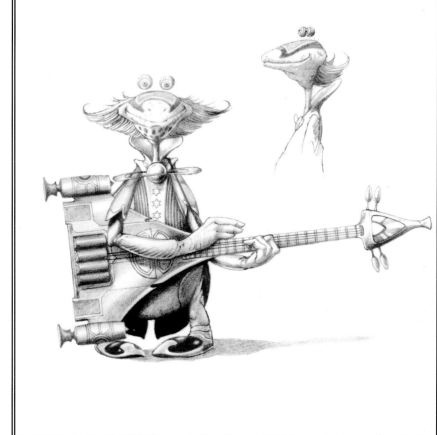

The main characters in the scenario have been fleshed out fairly thoroughly and it is tempting to introduce some of those shown here, but again paranoia bids caution.

The project is currently making a tour of prospective customers in the TV and film business, an exercise that can be recommended to anyone who feels that their patience could do with improving.

Above is shown the villain of the piece and, opposite, one of his vehicles, which demonstrates the common Matthews practice of using animal forms as the basis of his machines in order to trigger certain responses in the viewer. For instance, he says, if he had a mouse as the basis of this tank, the effect would have been rather different.

On the immediate right are examples of possible extra characters whose personalities and habits have not yet been explored.

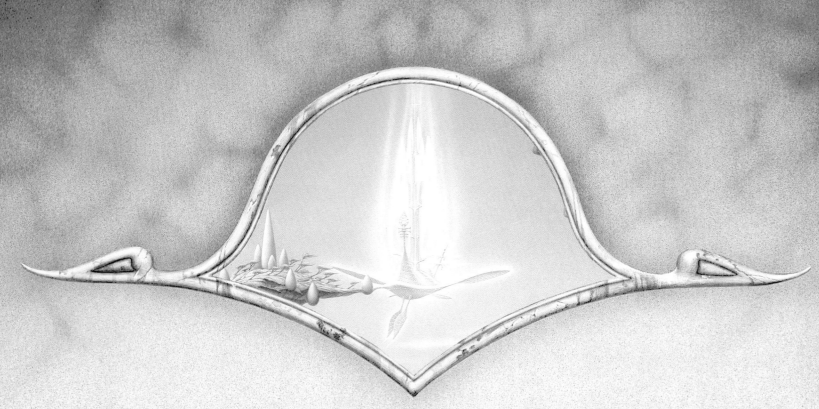

ACKNOWLEDGMENTS

Thanks to:
Karin my wife and Yendor my son
to Nigel for the text
Peter Ledeboer, Bob Moon, Paul Birch, Bristol Fine Art,
and to Tim Jones for help with the Sword of the Spirit.
Also thanks to
Dennis Elliott for the photo and loan of the coat!

Finally,
two texts which I remembered
while walking in the Welsh hills:

—

'Come to me, all you who are weary
and burdened, and I will give you rest . . .'
Matthew 11:28

—

'For God so loved the world that he gave
his only begotten Son,
that whoever believes in him shall not
perish but have eternal life . . .'
John 3:16